OCEAN LIFE UP CLOSE

Crabs

by Rebecca Pettiford

BELLWETHER MEDIA • MINNEAPOLIS, MN

Note to Librarians, Teachers, and Parents:

Blastoff! Readers are carefully developed by literacy experts and combine standards-based content with developmentally appropriate text.

Level 1 provides the most support through repetition of high-frequency words, light text, predictable sentence patterns, and strong visual support.

Level 2 offers early readers a bit more challenge through varied simple sentences, increased text load, and less repetition of high-frequency words.

Level 3 advances early-fluent readers toward fluency through increased text and concept load, less reliance on visuals, longer sentences, and more literary language.

Level 4 builds reading stamina by providing more text per page, increased use of punctuation, greater variation in sentence patterns, and increasingly challenging vocabulary.

Level 5 encourages children to move from "learning to read" to "reading to learn" by providing even more text, varied writing styles, and less familiar topics.

Whichever book is right for your reader, Blastoff! Readers are the perfect books to build confidence and encourage a love of reading that will last a lifetime!

This edition first published in 2017 by Bellwether Media, Inc.

No part of this publication may be reproduced in whole or in part without written permission of the publisher. For information regarding permission, write to Bellwether Media, Inc., Attention: Permissions Department, 5357 Penn Avenue South, Minneapolis, MN 55419.

Library of Congress Cataloging-in-Publication Data

Names: Pettiford, Rebecca, author.
Title: Crabs / by Rebecca Pettiford.
Description: Minneapolis, MN : Bellwether Media, Inc., [2017] | Series:
    Blastoff! Readers. Ocean Life Up Close | Audience: Ages 5-8. | Audience: K to
    grade 3. | Includes bibliographical references and index.
Identifiers: LCCN 2015045494 | ISBN 9781626174153 (hardcover : alk. paper)
Subjects: LCSH: Crabs–Juvenile literature.
Classification: LCC QL444.M33 P4755 2017 | DDC 595.3/86–dc23
LC record available at http://lccn.loc.gov/2015045494

Printed in the United States of America, North Mankato, MN.

Table of Contents

Crabs are **crustaceans**. Hard outer shells cover their wide bodies and protect them from danger.

shrimp

lobsters

barnacles

batwing
coral crab

Most crabs live in shallow
tide pools or on **coral reefs**.
Some live deep below the
ocean's surface.

The smallest crabs are less than 1 inch (2.5 centimeters) wide. The largest crabs can grow 13 feet (4 meters) from claw to claw!

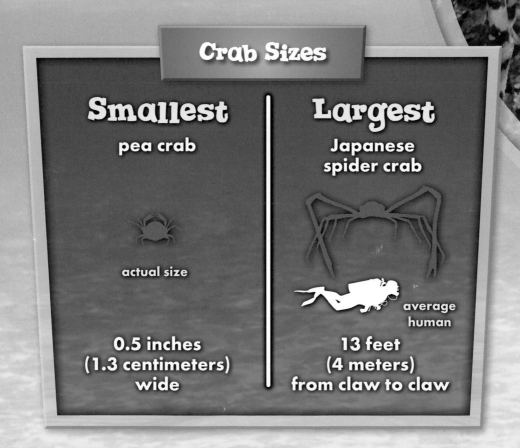

Crab Sizes

Smallest
pea crab

actual size

0.5 inches
(1.3 centimeters)
wide

Largest
Japanese
spider crab

average
human

13 feet
(4 meters)
from claw to claw

Japanese
spider crab

pea crab

pincer

fiddler
crab

Crabs use their ten legs to walk on land or the ocean floor. Some can even swim!

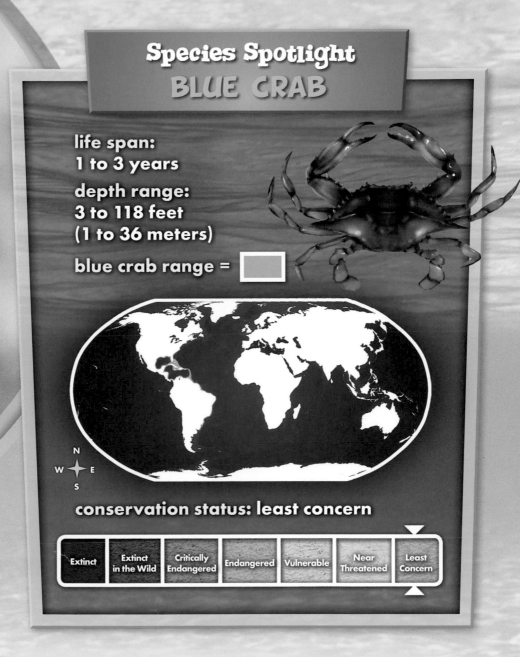

BLUE CRAB

life span:
1 to 3 years

depth range:
3 to 118 feet
(1 to 36 meters)

blue crab range =

N
W · E
S

conservation status: least concern

Extinct	Extinct in the Wild	Critically Endangered	Endangered	Vulnerable	Near Threatened	Least Concern

Their two front legs have claws called **pincers**. Crabs use their pincers to **grip** and crush food.

9

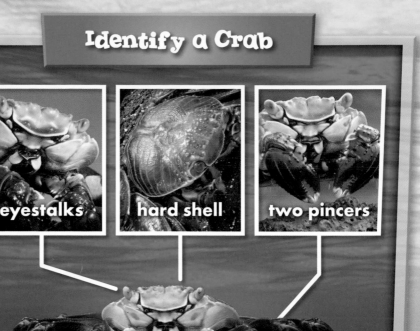

Identify a Crab

eyestalks

hard shell

two pincers

Crabs have two pairs of **antennae** on their heads. These help crabs feel, smell, and taste.

They have eyes at the ends of **eyestalks**. Their eyestalks can move in all directions.

eyestalk

antenna

horned
ghost crab

To grow, crabs must **molt**. Many crabs grow a new, soft shell under their hard shell. When the hard shell cracks, the crab wiggles free.

Other crabs do not make shells.
Instead, they live in the used shells
of other animals.

How Crabs Eat

Crabs are **omnivores**. They eat **algae** and small animals.

Crabs use their pincers to catch and hold **prey**. The pincers are strong enough to crush clamshells!

Catch of the Day

green algae

blue mussels

red sea urchins

rainbow crab

Hiding and Hatching

Many crabs bury themselves under sand to avoid **predators**. Some hide completely in their shells. Those with flat bodies can escape through narrow spaces.

If they cannot hide, crabs use their claws to fight off predators.

Sea Enemies

sea otters

ring-billed gulls

loggerhead sea turtles

boxer
crab

eggs

Female crabs can lay millions
of eggs. Newly hatched crabs
are called **larvae**.

The larvae look like tiny shrimp. They first float on the ocean surface and eat **plankton**.

Life Cycle of a Crab

egg

adult

larva

sponge
crab

The larvae molt many times.
After a few weeks, they look
like small crabs.

Soon they are ready for bigger shells and adventures!

porcelain crabs

Glossary

algae—plants and plantlike living things; most kinds of algae grow in water.

antennae—feelers on a crab's head that help it touch, smell, and taste

coral reefs—structures made of coral that usually grow in shallow seawater

crustaceans—animals that have several pairs of legs and hard outer shells; crabs and shrimp are types of crustaceans.

eyestalks—moveable stems that have an eye at each tip

grip—to hold tightly

larvae—early, tiny forms of an animal that must go through a big change to become an adult

molt—to shed a skin layer or shell so a new one can grow

omnivores—animals that eat both plants and animals

pincers—sharp, pointed claws

plankton—ocean plants or animals that drift in water; most plankton are tiny.

predators—animals that hunt other animals for food

prey—animals that are hunted by other animals for food

tide pools—seawater trapped by rocks on shore

To Learn More

AT THE LIBRARY

Howse, Jennifer. *Crabs*. New York, N.Y.: AV2 by Weigl, 2012.

Nagle, Kerry. *Crabs*. New York, N.Y.: Gareth Stevens Pub., 2010.

Wittrock, Jeni. *Pet Hermit Crabs Up Close*. North Mankato, Minn.: Capstone Press, 2015.

ON THE WEB

Learning more about crabs is as easy as 1, 2, 3.

1. Go to www.factsurfer.com.

2. Enter "crabs" into the search box.

3. Click the "Surf" button and you will see a list of related web sites.

With factsurfer.com, finding more information is just a click away.

Index

The images in this book are reproduced through the courtesy of: Yulia Vybornyh, front cover; NuntekulPhotography, p. 3; Sean Lema, pp. 4-5; Bennyartist, p. 5 (top); Atthapol Saita, p. 5 (center); Lia Caldas, p. 5 (bottom); Leonid Serebrennikov/ Age Fotostock/ SuperStock, p. 7 (top); mastersky, p. 7 (bottom); duangnapa_b, p. 8; Mikhail Kovalev, p. 9; Stubblefield Photography, p. 10 (top left); Eroom Niloc, p. 10 (top center); robert cicchetti, p. 10 (top right); MindStorm, p. 10 (bottom); Andrzej Grzegorczyk, p. 11; Tobias Bernhard Raff/ Corbis, p. 12; eye-blink, p. 13; Picturesbyme, p. 14; jcwait, p. 15 (top left); Kuttelvaserova Stuchelova, p. 15 (top center); Joe Belanger, p. 15 (top right); Irina Kozorog, p. 15 (bottom); Png Studio Photography, p. 17 (top left); Elliotte Rusty Harold, p. 17 (top center); Pete Niesen, p. 17 (top right); Piotr Naskrecki/ Minden Pictures/ SuperStock, p. 17 (bottom); Sphinx Wang, pp. 18, 19 (top); PhotosByChip, p. 19 (bottom left); Scenics & Science/ Alamy, p. 19 (bottom right); WaterFrame/ Alamy, pp. 20, 21.